# The Miracle of Christmas

## An Advent Study for Adults

## James W. Moore

ABINGDON PRESS / Nashville

THE MIRACLE OF CHRISTMAS
AN ADVENT STUDY FOR ADULTS

*Copyright © 2006 by Abingdon Press*

*This book is printed on acid-free paper.*

**Library of Congress Cataloging-in-Publication Data**

Moore, James W. (James Wendell), 1938-
    The miracle of Christmas : an Advent study for adults / James W. Moore.
        p. cm.
    ISBN: 0-687-33236-2 (binding: pbk., saddle-stitched -2 wires : alk. paper)
    1. Advent.    2. Christmas.    I. Title.

    BV40.M645 2006
    242'.33—dc22

                                                                2006022494

06 07 08 09 10 11 12 13 14 15—10 9 8 7 6 5 4 3 2 1
MANUFACTURED IN THE UNITED STATES OF AMERICA

*For Sarah, Paul, Dawson, and Daniel*

# Contents

# Introduction

One of the most beloved motion pictures in the history of filmmaking is the movie *Miracle on 34th Street*. Originally released in 1947 as a Christmas movie, it features Maureen O'Hara as a no-nonsense special-events executive for Macy's Department Store in New York, John Payne as a talented young lawyer, Natalie Wood as a bright and perceptive six-year-old girl, and Edmund Gwenn as a Macy's Santa who called himself Kris Kringle and insisted that he was the real Santa.

From the very beginning *Miracle on 34th Street* was well received, and over the years it has become an annual favorite, carrying the tagline, "Capture the spirit of Christmas with this timeless classic." It's a sweet-spirited movie about the miracle of Christmas. When I was a young boy, it was one of my favorite movies, but even then I knew what I know now: that the real miracle of Christmas, the most important Christmas Miracle, happened in a manger in Bethlehem long ago.

There, God came in the birth of Jesus to visit and redeem his people.

There, God entered into history to do for us what we cannot do for ourselves—to save us!

There, through a little baby born in a lowly stable, God's will, God's idea, God's intention, God's Word, God's purpose, and God's love became flesh and blood and lived among us, full of grace and truth.

There, through this lowly birth, God brought salvation to the world, inspiring the Gospel writer to later write these words:

> For God so loved the world that he gave his only Son, so that everyone who believes in him may not perish but may have eternal life. (John 3:16)

This is the real miracle of Christmas—the miracle of God's seeking, saving love for each one of us.

In this book, as we journey together through the four Sundays of Advent back to the manger in Bethlehem, we will discover "The Miracle of Good News," "The Miracle of Hospitality," "The Miracle of Giving," and "The Miracle of Christmas."

# The Miracle of Good News

*Scripture: Read Luke 1:39-45.*

His name was Joey. Joey was nine years old and in the fourth grade. He was so excited because his teacher, Miss Thompson, had chosen him to be in the annual Christmas play. Joey was going to be one of the Christmas angels, and he was more than a little nervous, because he had a speaking part in the play, and memorizing lines was not his strong suit. He had only one line, but Miss Thompson told him that it was one of the most important lines in the whole story.

Joey was to play the angel of Christmas, and at the most dramatic moment in the pageant, he was to say, "Behold, I bring you glad tidings of great joy." This was a problem for Joey, because he didn't know what those words meant. He had never in his whole life said the word *behold*, and the words *glad tidings* were also not to be found anywhere in his nine-year-old vocabulary.

Miss Thompson sensed Joey's frustration, and she said to him, "Joey, simply imagine that you have just heard the most wonderful news, and you have run to tell your friends all about it. That's what 'Behold, I bring you glad tidings of great joy' means." Joey took in her explanation, and he went to work. Finally he mastered the line, and he could say it with dramatic flair and boldness, "Behold, I bring you glad tidings of great joy!"

And when the night of the big performance came, Joey was ready. At least, he was ready until the curtains opened and he saw all those people out there, and then there were those bright spotlights shining directly in his face. Joey got a classic case of stage fright, and his mind went completely blank. For the life of him, he could not remember his line. Not a word of it. But he did remember what Miss Thompson had told him about running to tell his friends some wonderful news, so when it came time for his line, instead of saying, "Behold, I bring you glad tidings of great joy!" Joey blurted out, "Boy, oh boy, do I have good news for *you!*" The audience laughed loudly and gave Joey a standing ovation.

Now, a few people got upset with Joey, because they felt that he had ruined the Christmas play. But more (many, many more) loved it and felt that Joey's blurted-out words were the highlight of the pageant, and that through a little child it had happened—Christmas had come once again!

Joey's unusual performance actually happened years ago, but to this day in that community, when the people gather for the annual Christmas play, they all talk about Joey and how on that night long ago Joey got the words wrong but the spirit right when he shouted out with great enthusiasm, "Boy, oh boy, do I have good news for *you!*"

Well, Joey was right, wasn't he? Christmas does have good news for us, incredible news, amazing news, the greatest news this world has ever heard.

Christmas also has some wonderful lessons about life to teach us. We see that, for example, in the first chapter of Luke's Gospel in this beautiful scene where Mary, who is to become the mother of Jesus, goes to visit her older cousin Elizabeth, who also is expecting. Elizabeth, even though she is quite old to be having a baby, will soon miraculously deliver a baby boy who will grow up to be John the Baptist, the forerunner of the Messiah, the one who will prepare the way for the coming of Jesus Christ. God blessed both Mary and Elizabeth with miracle births, that he might bless the world with the miracle of Christmas.

Notice this: God first sends an angel to Elizabeth and her husband, Zechariah, then to Mary and Joseph, then to the shepherds, and in each case, the angel says, in essence, "Boy, oh boy, do I have good news for *you!*"

Now, let's look at this poignant passage in Luke 1 in which these two expectant mothers (one quite old and one quite young) get together to talk about the miraculous things that are happening, and to affirm and support each other. Boy, oh boy, is there good news here for you and me! Let me show you what I mean.

## First of All, Look at the Good News of Christmas Found in the Faith of Mary

Her strong, unflinching, unwavering faith is amazing. Some years ago, Kenny Rogers came out with a new Christmas song called "Mary, Did You Know?" It's a pensive, contemplative song with a poignant, haunting melody. The composer is asking Mary if she really knew and understood the amazing thing that was happening. Did she really comprehend who her baby boy was? Did she realize what her Son would do in the world and for the world? Did she know already the good he would do, the miracles he would perform, the good news he would bring? And then the song concludes with these powerful words: "[Mary] did you know that your baby boy is heaven's perfect Lamb? / This sleeping child you're holding is the great I AM?"

Well, what do you think? How much did Mary know? Let's go back to the story in Luke and find out.

There is so much to learn from Mary. She has so much to teach us about real faith. When we see her so beautifully portrayed in Christmas pageants and on Christmas cards and in Nativity scenes, she looks so serene and lovely and the whole matter appears so simple and easy.

But—think realistically about it for a moment. Consider realistically what Mary went through. It must have been incredibly difficult:

• the whisperings behind her back
• the finger-pointing
• the false accusations
• the raised eyebrows
• the questions
• the gossip
• the criticism
• the family pressures
• the crude jokes
• the cruel laughter
• the poverty

11

• the heavy taxes, not to mention the hard journey back to Joseph's place of birth, mandated by the census at a time when an expectant mother shouldn't have had to travel anywhere (see Luke 2:1-7)
• the birth in a stable, with no doctor, no midwife, no medicine, and no anesthetic
• nothing, but faith in God!

Mary was just a teenaged girl from a poor family who lived in an obscure village, which itself was under the rule of a despised foreign power. Then one day, out of the blue, an angel came to her with a message from the Lord, "Do not be afraid, Mary, for you have found favor with God. And behold, you will conceive in your womb and bear a son, and you shall call his name Jesus. He will be great, and will be called the Son of the Most High" (Luke 1:30-32 RSV). And all of this was going to happen without Mary's ever being intimate with any man.

Now, be honest. Would you have believed that? The remarkable thing is that Mary did! That's real faith, isn't it? She was willing to hear God's word, obey God's will, and entrust the future in God's hands, even though it put her in an awkward, difficult, complicated situation. How would she explain this? How would she communicate this to her parents? How would she tell Joseph? They were legally betrothed. They had not yet consummated their marriage, but they were considered as good as married, and in those days when you became formally engaged as they were, the only way you could be separated was through divorce. How could she tell Joseph that she was going to have a baby, and how would he handle it? And what would the neighbors say?

It was a tough situation for Mary, and most of us would have asked the Lord to find someone else to do this job. But not Mary. She did not know what was ahead for her and her son—not a lot of specifics, not a lot of details—but her answer to the angel was a model of real faith, "I am the handmaid of the Lord," she said. "Let it be to me according to your word" (Luke 1:38 RSV). Or in other words, what Mary said was, "I am the Lord's servant. O Lord, thy will be done. Use me, O Lord, as you will. I trust you completely." What a powerful portrait of faith we see in Mary!

Let me ask you something. Do you have faith like that? Can you say, "Thy will be done, O Lord," and really mean it, really trust God like Mary did? Is your faith that strong? That's something to think about, isn't it?

The faith of Mary: that's number one.

## Second, Look at the Good News of Christmas in the Encouragement of Elizabeth

In Luke 1, when Mary comes to visit her older cousin Elizabeth, isn't it beautiful how Elizabeth responds? No jealousy, no skepticism, no cynicism, no suspicious questions—just loving affirmation, positive reinforcement, an "I love you," "I'm so happy for you," "I'm so proud of you," "I'm here for you" (see Luke 1:39-45, 56). We all need someone like that.

When I was a teenager, my older cousin Marie filled that role for me. She was twenty-five years older than me, and no matter what, she was always glad to see me, always glad to listen to me, always loving, always upbeat, always affirming, always encouraging. I could bring my joys and sorrows, my victories and disappointments to Marie, and I knew before I said a word just how she would respond—with love and encouragement. I have wonderful memories of Marie and her wisdom, the ways in which she always gave me the positive reinforcement I needed.

Some years ago at a university in the Midwest, some students in a psychology class were studying the power of positive reinforcement, the impact it has on a person when you give encouragement, and the debilitating effect that comes when positive reinforcement is withheld. The psychology professor was called out of the room for a few moments one day. Now, leaving psychology students alone even for a few minutes is risky business, as the professor soon found out. The students decided to have some fun with the professor and, at the same time, to test his theories about positive reinforcement.

The professor was in the habit of pacing back and forth across the front of the classroom as he lectured. So the students decided, without the professor's knowledge, to do this: every time the professor moved toward the radiator in the classroom, they would give him dramatic positive reinforcement. They would say, "Yes! All right! Amen!" They would applaud and smile and nod and take notes like crazy. With verbal expression and body language they affirmed and encouraged him as he walked toward the radiator.

But when he moved away from the radiator, the students would do the opposite. They would moan and groan and yawn and stretch and put their pencils down. They would look out the window or nod off as though they were about to fall asleep, and they would look and act as if they were bored to tears. Now, they never told the professor what they were doing, and he never figured it out. But by the end of the week, he was giving his entire lecture sitting on the radiator!

We all need it, positive reinforcement, and this is one of the great messages of Christmas. God, through the gift of the Christ Child, reaches out to us with love and encouragement and affirmation, and he wants us to live in that spirit, as Elizabeth did. God wants us to celebrate one another and to give one another the positive reinforcement, love, and encouragement we all need.

How is it with you right now? Are you a child of faith like Mary? Are you a child of encouragement like Elizabeth?

## Third and Finally, Look at the Good News of Christmas in the Action of God

The gracious, loving, forgiving, seeking, saving action of God: This is the good news of Christmas! God will not give up on us. God will not desert us. God will not let us go. God comes to where we are, looking for us with his amazing grace and his sacrificial, redemptive love.

In 1989 an earthquake hit Armenia, and over 25,000 people lost their lives. One area hit especially hard had an elementary school in it. After the tremors had stopped, a father of one of the students raced to the school to check on his son. When the father arrived on the scene, he was stunned to see that the school building had been leveled. Looking at the mass of stones and rubble, he remembered a promise he had made to his little boy, Arman. He had told him, "No matter what happens, Arman, I'll always be there for you." Remembering his promise, he found the area closest to his son's classroom and began to pull back the rocks. Others had also come, and they said to the man, "It's too late. You know they are all gone. No one could survive that! You can't help them now." Even a policeman urged him to give up and go on home.

But that father refused to quit. For eight hours, then sixteen, then thirty-two, and then thirty-six hours, he continued to dig through the rubble. His hands were raw and his energy gone, but he would not give up. Finally, after thirty-eight wrenching hours, he pulled back a boulder, and he heard voices. He recognized his son's voice. He called out to him, "Arman! Arman!" And a voice answered him, "Dad, it's me!" And then the boy said, "I told the other kids not to worry. I told them you would come save us because you promised, 'No matter what, I'll always be there for you.' I knew you would never give up."

This is the good news of Christmas, isn't it? God comes into the rubble of our lives and seeks us out and saves us. We see the miracle of Christmas in the faith of Mary and in the encouragement of Elizabeth, but most of all, we see it in the saving action of God.

## Questions for Reflection and Discussion

1. Share your definition of *good news*, and describe how it feels to be able to share good news with others.
2. In your own words, describe Mary. In what ways did she demonstrate her faith in God's plan?
3. What can we learn from Elizabeth about giving encouragement to others? Who has been a source of encouragement in your life?
4. How have you experienced the saving action of God in your life, or where have you seen it in the lives of others?
5. What does the good news of Christmas mean to you? In what ways do you share the good news of Christmas?

## Prayer

Dear God, thank you for miracles, and for being able to share the good news of Jesus with others. Help us grow in faith and in love. Prepare our hearts for the birth of Jesus, that we may experience the joy and blessings of Christmas. Amen.

## Focus for the Week

Begin your observance of Advent by contemplating the tidings of great joy that arrive each Christmas. How are you transformed by the birth of Jesus? Is there evidence of joy in your daily life? Think about the good news of the Savior's birth each day this week, and consider ways you can share that good news with others.

# The Miracle of Hospitality

*Scripture: Read Luke 2:1-7.*

It was Christmas Eve. A man was waiting for a bus to take him from Athens, Georgia, to Greenville, South Carolina. As he purchased his ticket, the agent said, "That bus is running a little late. If you'll just watch the electronic letterboard over there in the corner, you will know when the bus arrives and when it's time to board."

The man wandered around the terminal for a while. Eventually he saw a small machine. The sign on the machine read, "For twenty-five cents, this machine will tell you your name, age, city of residence, and something about you."

"That's impossible," the man muttered out loud, but nevertheless he was curious, so he pulled out a quarter and plunked it into the machine. The machine whirred and whistled a bit, and then printed out a message that read, "Your name is Fred Jones. You are thirty-five years old. You live in Athens, Georgia, and you are waiting for a bus to Greenville, South Carolina."

"Incredible," said the man. "How does that machine know all of that? It's amazing, but I'll bet it can't do it again." So he plunked in another quarter. Again, the machine whirred and whistled for a bit, and then out came the message, "Your name is Fred Jones. You are thirty-five years old. You live in Athens, Georgia, and you are *still* waiting for a bus to Greenville, South Carolina."

"This cannot be happening!" the man exclaimed. He put on some sunglasses, mussed his hair a bit, turned the collar up on his jacket,

17

and tried another quarter. The response came back: "Your name is still Fred Jones. You are still thirty-five years old. You still live in Athens, Georgia, and for the third time, you are *still* waiting for a bus to Greenville, South Carolina."

The man was amazed. He glanced across the street and saw a novelty shop. He walked out of the bus terminal, crossed the street, and went into the store. There he bought a pair of glasses with a large nose attached, a shaggy gray wig, a baggy shirt, and a cane. He then hobbled back across the street, acting like a much older man, and he walked up to the machine. He put a fourth quarter into the slot. The machine whirred and groaned and whistled, and then put out a message that read, "Your name is Fred Jones. You are thirty-five years old. You live in Athens, Georgia; and while you were horsing around, you missed your bus to Greenville, South Carolina!"

This story is a Christmas parable for us, and the message is this: Sometimes when we are waiting for Christmas, we horse around so much—we *busy* ourselves so much—that we miss the very thing we are waiting for. Sometimes we get so involved in the tasks and details of Christmas that we forget the One we are honoring. Five little words in the Gospel of Luke say it all: "No room in the inn" (Luke 2:7 NIV, adapted).

There is a certain pathos in those words, "No room for you here." That was the beginning of the Master's life. That was the very first thing the world said to Jesus Christ. That experience would plague him the remainder of his days on this earth and indeed even to this present moment. "No room!" "We're just too crowded!" "Sorry, we are full up!" "Try again some other time!" "No room for you here, so if you'll excuse me, I've got a million and one things to see about!" "It's too bad, but there's just no room."

Let's be honest now; isn't this our problem, yours and mine? We get so busy, so tired, so preoccupied with the incessant demands on our crowded and hectic lives that we shut out the very birth of the Master we so long to know.

Some years ago, I ran across a poem that says it well. The poem suggests we are very much like that little inn in Bethlehem at the first Christmas. Our lives, too, get so crowded and so filled up that we don't have room for Christ. The poem concludes with these poignant lines: "[Like the Bethlehem inn] we have no hostile feeling, / We merely crowd him out."

Christmas brings us good news, that unto us a Savior is given. Christmas also brings to each one of us a haunting question, namely this: *Do you have room in your heart for Christ?* Well, do you? If you don't have Christmas in your heart, you are not likely to find it under your tree.

One of the most famous and beloved paintings in the world today is Holman Hunt's painting "The Light of the World." In the painting, Jesus is not a baby. He is depicted as the resurrected Christ. He holds a lantern in his hand, which is a symbol of salvation. Jesus is knocking at the door—the door of a human heart. But there is one small detail most people don't notice at first. There is no latch on the outside; the door can be opened only from within. In other words, only you can let the light of God's love, incarnate in Jesus, into your heart.

Won't you let him in? Won't you offer him your warmest hospitality? Won't you welcome him into your life this year with open arms? Won't you receive him into your life as never before? Won't you make room for him? This is the haunting question of Christmas: *Do you have room in your heart for Jesus Christ?*

Let me bring this closer to home by raising three questions. Here is question number one.

## First, Do You Have Room in Your Heart for Faith in Christ?

A man and a woman were standing on the corner of 5$^{th}$ Avenue and 57$^{th}$ Street in New York City. It was Christmastime, and the Christmas rush was going on in full force before their very eyes. They were waiting for the traffic light to change. The man obviously was irritated by the crowds, the hubbub, and the traffic. In frustration, he growled, "This town is totally disorganized. Look at this traffic! What a mess! It's terrible! Awful! Something ought to be done about it. It's just ridiculous!"

The woman, on the other hand, had a different view altogether. She responded to his outburst by saying, "You know, when you really stop to think about it, it's not ridiculous at all. It's amazing! It's astonishing! The romance of it is extraordinary! There was a baby boy born in a peasant family in a little out-of-the-way village halfway around the world from here. The parents had no money, no clout, no prestige, no social standing, yet 2,000 years later, their little baby creates a traffic jam on 5<sup>th</sup> Avenue, one of the most sophisticated streets in the world. This irritates you? It should fascinate you! It should amaze you! It should thrill you! It should inspire you!"

I don't know about you, but I wholeheartedly agree with that woman. You see, we don't have to choose between Bethlehem and "Bedlam." Bethlehem always happens in the midst of our Bedlam. Those who have the eyes of faith can see it, those who have the ears of faith can hear it, and those who have hearts of faith can feel it and celebrate it. You may find this strange for anyone to say, but I love the happy chaos of Christmas, because it reminds me of the incredible impact of Christ on this world.

But let me ask you this: *Has Christ made an impact on your personal life? Has he made a dramatic impact on your soul, your heart, your actions, and your decisions?* Commitment to Christ, accepting Christ into your life, knowing Christ as your Savior; that is an intensely personal thing. No one else can do it for us, because Christianity is not just mouthing a creed; it is knowing a *person*. When Paul wrote his letter to Timothy, he did not say, "I know *what* I have believed." Rather, he said, "I know *whom* I have believed" (2 Timothy 1:12 NIV, emphasis added).

One of the saddest things I ever witnessed in my life occurred some years ago when I was a student pastor. A man in my church died because he refused to take penicillin. He had what started out as a minor infection. The doctor examined him and assured him that he could be healed quite quickly by this amazing miracle medicine, penicillin, but he was suspicious of what he called "these new-fangled ideas," and he would not take the medicine. The doctors reasoned with him, the nurses pled with him, and his family begged him to try it, but no luck. He would not give in.

I told the man about my own experience with penicillin (once when I had appendicitis, and another time when I was spiked in the leg in a baseball game and the wound became infected). I related to him how quick and painless and effective the penicillin had been for me. We prayed with him about it. We gave him convincing materials to read that documented the incredible healing powers of penicillin. But still he refused, and then it was too late. He would not take the penicillin, and he died. Tragically, sadly, unnecessarily, he died because he would not receive the medicine that would make him well.

Isn't that sad? Isn't that heartbreaking? I gladly would have taken the penicillin for him. So would his wife and his mother and his daughters and his doctors, but we couldn't. We could not do it for him. He needed to do it personally.

Faith is like that; no one else can do it for you. People can tell you about Christ and his power to heal and save. They can give you convincing materials. They can beg you and plead with you, and pray and reason with you, and encourage you. But in the final analysis, it is so intensely personal—a personal decision to accept Christ into your life as your Lord and Savior, to receive him within.

So the first question is, do you have room in your heart for faith in Christ?

## Second, Do You Have Room in Your Heart for Hope in Christ?

Some years ago, there was a plane crash in the mountains. The plane smashed into the side of a mountain, slid down a glacier, and came to rest just short of a dangerous precipice. Most of the passengers died on impact. Others died later from their injuries. But sixteen people survived the crash and hung on for two months high up in the mountains, hoping and praying that soon someone would find them and rescue them.

It was a horrible, horrendous experience, and toward the end of the two-month period most all of them had given up and lost all hope. "If they were going to find us, they would have found us by now."

But three men volunteered to go and see if they could find a way out. They started out walking at 15,000-foot elevation in rugged terrain, in ice and snow. One of the men got discouraged and turned back. Two others kept going. They walked for ten days until they came to a swollen river. They could not cross it. It was too dangerous. They wondered, *Is this the end? Is there any hope for us now?*

They camped there for the night. The next morning, they saw a man standing on the other side of the river. They stood up, waved their arms, and yelled to him. The man just stared back at them. Then he turned and walked away. The next morning he was back again. Once again they yelled and waved their arms. This time the man took a piece of paper out of his pocket, tied it to a stone and threw it across the river. They rushed over to where it had landed,

21

opened it up, and read the words, "There is a man coming that I told to come"; in other words, the note was saying help is on the way.

Then the man took a chunk of bread out of his pocket and threw it across the river. One of the survivors held the chunk of bread in his hand as if it were a sign, a sacrament that said, "Someone has heard our cries and cares; someone knows about us; someone will come and lead us out of here." The man turned to his companion and said, "We are saved!"

That is the hope of Christmas, the hope of our Christian faith. Someone knows about us, someone has heard our cries and cares. Someone has come and will come to save us and redeem us and deliver us. The Christmas story in the Bible puts it like this: "You shall call his name Jesus, for he will save his people" (Matthew 1:21 RSV).

But the question for you and me is this: *Do you know that kind of hope? Do you have room in your heart for faith in Christ, and do you have room in your heart for hope in Christ?*

## Third and Finally, Do You Have Room in Your Heart for Love in Christ?

Christian love is more than just loving those who look like us and dress like us and act like us. It is more than just loving those who love us back. It is loving all people because they are God's children. It means loving every person we meet for God's sake.

A good friend of mine tells a true story that makes the point. It happened on a Saturday morning. He was sitting at the kitchen table with his coffee when his son Mark walked in. Mark was sniffling, and my friend thought, *Oh no, Mark is coming down with a cold.*

But then he saw that it wasn't a cold; Mark was crying and holding his hands cupped together out in front of him. Tears were streaming down his face. Mark opened his hands, and there was the lifeless form of Mark's little pet hamster. It had died during the night, and Mark's heart was broken. At this point, my friend digresses to say, "Now, I don't like hamsters. I don't care for them at all. They sleep during the day and run around on that squeaking wheel all night. But there in that moment, all the love I had went out to that little hamster. Why? Because Mark loved him, so I loved him too, for Mark's sake."

Christian love is like that. It seeks people out and loves them because God loves them; it loves them for God's sake; it loves them

22

because they are precious to God. This is why Jesus came into the world in such a humble way, to show dramatically and graphically God's love for all people, and to teach us how to love one another unconditionally, as God loves us.

Well, what do you think? How is it with you right now? Do you have room in your heart for faith in Christ? Do you have room in your heart for hope in Christ? Do you have room in your heart for love in Christ? That's something to think about, isn't it, as we move toward Christmas.

## Questions for Reflection and Discussion

1. Explain what it means to offer Jesus (and others) your warmest hospitality.
2. Discuss the author's statement that "Christianity is not just mouthing a creed; it is knowing a *person.*" Describe how things change when you come to know Christ.
3. What are some ways you can make more room in your heart for faith in Christ?
4. Share what having hope in Christ means to you, and relate it to an experience from your life.
5. Reflect on or discuss the idea that Christian love means loving all people because they are God's children. How is this idea connected to Christmas?

## Prayer

Dear God, thank you for showing us how to open our hearts to Jesus. Help us make room for more faith, more hope, and more love as we continue our Advent journey. Show us how to act as servants as we offer our love and hospitality to others, that they may see in us the joy of knowing Jesus. Amen.

## Focus for the Week

Reflect on how well you practice hospitality. Think about ways to make more room for others, and consider performing a daily act of hospitality. Don't get so caught up in the details of Christmas planning that you forget to celebrate and cherish those people whom God has placed in your life. Remember what Jesus has given you, and think about what you can give to others.

# The Miracle of Giving

*Scripture: Read Matthew 2:1-12.*

Timmy and Jack were best buddies, young boys who were next-door neighbors growing up together. They were together every day. They were the same age and in the same class at school and in church. They did everything together. They were both excellent students and outstanding athletes. Timmy and Jack were like brothers, but they were extremely competitive with each other.

In school, they would always run against each other for class president. One year Timmy would win, and the next year Jack would win, and so it went. One year Jack would have the best grades, and the next year Timmy would.

In football, they were both so talented that on one series Timmy would play quarterback and Jack would play tailback, and on the next series, they would switch positions. And when they played basketball in the backyard, one-on-one against each other, it was all-out battle. The competition was fierce.

When they reached the fifth grade, it came time for the Christmas play, and Jack wanted to play the role of Joseph. He had played Joseph the year before and had received lots of compliments on his performance and he wanted to do it again. But the teacher said, "Jack, you played Joseph last year. Let's let Timmy be Joseph this year, and you can be the innkeeper." Jack was not amused, and he decided on the night of the play that he would play a trick on Timmy; he would get Timmy, but good!

So during the play, as Mary and Joseph approached the innkeeper, Timmy, playing the role of Joseph, said his lines perfectly, "Sir, can you help us? As you can see, Mary is about to have her baby. She is so tired from our long journey. We need lodging. I know the city is crowded right now, but please, sir, can you help us?"

This was the moment Jack had been waiting and planning for. This was the moment where Jack could play his trick and put one over on his friend Timmy. So Jack, playing the innkeeper, said loudly and dramatically, "Can I help you? Absolutely, I can! Come right on in, Mary and Joseph. You can have the bridal suite!" There was a stunned pause as Timmy tried to figure out what to do and what to say to keep the Christmas play going.

Timmy was accustomed to matching wits with Jack, though, so pretty quickly he came up with the answer. He walked up to Jack, the innkeeper, peered over his shoulder, and then said, "Look at the place, Mary. It's a disgrace! I wouldn't stay in this dump for anything! Come on, Mary. We'd be better off in a stable than in a place like this!" Now *that's* what you call rising to the occasion. Timmy rose to the occasion and kept the Christmas story going.

Rising to the occasion: that's precisely what the wise men in Luke 2 did.

They rose to the occasion by seeing the star and then following the star as it led them to the Christ Child.

They rose to the occasion by taking the time and coming up with the financial support needed to make the long, arduous, and expensive journey.

They rose to the occasion by bringing gifts that not only were appropriate for the celebration of the birth of the Christ Child, but also gifts that foreshadowed who the Christ Child would become and what he would do.

First, there was gold, a gift fit for a king, an appropriate gift for this one who was the King of kings and who would choose to reign not with force but with love.

Second, there was frankincense, a gift fit for a priest. In the temple in those days, the sweet perfume of frankincense was used. By the way, the Latin word for *priest* is *ponifex*, which literally means "bridge-builder." Jesus would become the One who builds a bridge between God and us and makes it possible for us to enter into the presence of God.

And third, there was the gift of myrrh. Myrrh was used for embalming, so myrrh was a gift fit for one who had come to die for us.

The famous artist William Holman Hunt once created a painting that shows Jesus as a young man, standing in a doorway stretching his arm after working in the carpenter shop all day. He stands there in the doorway with his arms outstretched, and behind him, on the wall, the setting sun casts his shadow, and it is the shadow of a cross! The gifts presented that day by the wise men foretold that Jesus was to be the true King of kings, the Priest who bridges us to God, and the Savior who dies on the cross to save us from our sins.

The wise men rose to the occasion and played their part beautifully. But there was another way they rose to the occasion, one that was even more daring and courageous: they defied King Herod. In order to save the Christ Child's life, they disobeyed King Herod, and that was a dangerous thing to do indeed, because King Herod was a powerful, dangerous, coldhearted man.

He was called "Herod the Great," and in some ways he was a great ruler. He ruled as king for nearly thirty-five years, and during that time, he did succeed in keeping the peace. And he was a great builder; he was responsible for rebuilding the temple in Jerusalem. But Herod had one huge problem: he was insanely afraid that he might lose his kingdom. The longer Herod lived, the worse his fear became. His solution was to eliminate anybody who might become a threat to his throne, so, over the years he executed his wife, his mother-in-law, three of his own sons, and many others, including John the Baptist.

To give you a glimpse into the coldhearted, self-centered nature of Herod, look at what he did when he was seventy years old. He knew that he would not live much longer, so he issued the order that at the precise moment of his death, a large collection of the most distinguished and respected citizens of Jerusalem should be executed. By this action, he tried to dupe history. He knew that when the word went out that these beloved community leaders had been killed, there would be great grief and mourning and crying in the streets, and that when future historians would look back at this moment, they might mistakenly think that the tears of the people were being shed for Herod. Luckily, this command was not carried out!

But when we think of Herod and his warped and selfish way of thinking, then we can imagine how he must have felt when he heard that a child was to be born in Bethlehem, and that the child was destined to become the king of the Jews. Herod told the wise men to go to Bethlehem and find the baby and then to notify him so that he, too, could come and worship the baby. But, you see, the wise men really were *wise* men—they saw through Herod and his plot. So after they found the Christ Child and presented their gifts, the wise men disobeyed King Herod's order; they didn't report back to him the location of the baby, because they knew that Herod didn't want to worship the baby; he wanted to kill the baby.

The wise men not only were wise, they were also brave. So, we could say (not counting Mary and Joseph) that the wise men were the first people in the world to give gifts to the Christ Child, and the first ones in the world to take a courageous and bold stand for Jesus.

Now, obviously we can't go back to that night in Bethlehem and bring gifts to the manger, but what can we give to Jesus? What can you and I give him today? What can you and I give him right now?

In 1872, Christina Rossetti wrote a beautiful poem about this, which contains these poignant words:

> What can I give him,
> Poor as I am?
> If I were a shepherd,
> I would bring a lamb;
> If I were a Wise Man,
> I would do my part;
> Yet what I can I give him:
> Give my heart.
> (from "In the Bleak Midwinter")

Now, with this as a backdrop for our thinking, let me suggest three good gifts that we can give the Christ Child for Christmas this year.

## First of All, We Can Bring Him Our Penitence

Here is where we start—with penitence, with sorrow for our sins. This is what the Advent and Christmas seasons underscore for us so dramatically, how very much we need a Savior.

You see, this world is not enough. Apart from God, we are incomplete. We have sinned. We can't make it by ourselves. We need help. We desperately need a Savior. That's what Advent and Christmas tell us.

Recently a young man filled out an application form for admission to college. One of the questions read, "What are your personal strengths?" The young man wrote, "Sometimes I'm trustworthy, loyal, cooperative, and kind." Then the form said, "List your weaknesses," and he wrote, "Sometimes I'm not trustworthy, loyal, cooperative, or kind." We all can relate to that, can't we? And that's why we approach the manger of Christmas on our knees in the spirit of penitence.

Have you ever been to the city of Bethlehem? In the city is a small cathedral at the supposed birthplace of Jesus. Inside the church is a small cave lit by lamps. In the tile floor is a star design that marks where the manger was. Visitors are allowed inside the sacred cave, but you cannot walk in with your head and shoulders held high. The door is so low that you must stoop to enter.

There's a sermon there somewhere, and I think it is this: you may be able to see the world standing tall and proud, but to witness the Savior, you have to get on your knees. You come in humility and penitence.

Max Lucado, in his book *The Applause of Heaven,* puts it like this: "While the theologians were sleeping and the elite were dreaming and the successful were snoring, the meek and penitent were kneeling. They were kneeling before the One only the meek and penitent will see. They were kneeling in front of Jesus" (p. 73).

Someone once gave us a Christmas card that says it all. The card has the caption, "God Sent Us a Saviour" and it lists the options God had in sending salvation to the world. Should He send an educator? Or a scientist? Or an entertainer? No! Our greatest need was not information or technology or pleasure. The card concludes with these powerful words: "Our greatest need was forgiveness, so God sent us a Saviour!"

This is the good news of Christmas. We needed a Savior, and God sent us one. Talk about exchanging gifts for Christmas!

First of all, we bring God our penitence, and he will give us the gift of salvation and life.

## *Second, We Can Bring Him Our Gratitude*

Some years ago there was a little girl whose name was Jane. She was one of six children living with her family in East Texas. Suddenly,

29

Jane's father became ill with heart problems so serious that he would not be able to work for some time. Jane knew that the family would be in for a lot of changes, and sure enough, her mother told her the news. "I'm so sorry, Jane," her mother said. "I know school is about to start, but right now there is no money for school clothes and supplies." Jane was shocked. No school supplies? No new school clothes? All her old clothes were too small, but she could tell by her mother's face that it was a serious situation.

"We hope and pray that Dad will be better soon," Jane's mother went on to say. "He can't work now, so we all have to pitch in and help. We all will have to help earn money for food." So the children took odd jobs. Jane worked at the neighborhood store, her brother took a newspaper route, another sister worked at the grocery store, and another babysat.

One day the phone rang. It was the church secretary. "I know school is starting soon. Some people here at the church want to help Jane. They are going to buy her some new clothes for school and all of her school supplies." Jane couldn't believe it. The clothes were better than she could have imagined, and the school supplies were just right.

Jane and her mother were so grateful, and they wanted to say thank you to the people who had helped them so graciously and so generously. They called the church. Jane's mother said, "Could you help us? We want to say thank you to the kind people who did so much for Jane." The church secretary replied, "The people who helped you said you can thank them by just doing something kind for someone else."

Well, over the years Jane and her mother have done just that. When Jane's father's health improved, Jane's mother began to take meals to people who were sick at home, and she continued to do so for many years. Not too long ago, Jane's mother was honored by the Meals on Wheels program for twenty-five years of delivering meals to people who were not able to leave their home. And Jane became so committed to helping other people as an expression of her gratitude that when she grew up, she went into full-time Christian service, and she is now a member of our staff who helps children and families every single day. Her name is Jane Williams. She is our director of children's and family ministries at St. Luke's Church here in Houston. Jane was so grateful to God and to the church that she committed her life to serving God and to helping other people.

That's what it means to be a Christian. We are so grateful to God for his gift of Jesus Christ that we can't sit still. We want to pass it on, to pay it forward, to share it with others as an expression of our thanksgiving to God for what God has done for us in sending Christ into the world.

When we really understand and accept and wrap our arms around and celebrate that, it changes our lives. It makes us grateful servants.

First, we bring to the Christ Child the gift of penitence. And second, we bring the gift of gratitude.

## Third and Finally, We Can Bring to the Christ Child Our Love for Others

That's what Jesus wants most of all. Remember how he said it: "As you did it to one of the least of these . . . you did it to me" (Matthew 25:40). Nothing makes glad the heart of Christ more than when he sees us love one another.

A few years ago, noted minister and author Dr. Hoover Rupert told about a beautiful incident that took place at the Mohawk Central School in Pains Hollow, New York. The principal of that school became concerned that some of the children whose families were struggling financially would have no Christmas. So he set up a Santa's Helpers Fund and encouraged all the students who could to contribute to it, so that gifts might be bought for the underprivileged children in the area.

One thirteen-year-old boy was touched by the idea, and he scrimped and saved for weeks so that he could help some poor child have a gift for Christmas that year. The boy managed to raise fifteen cents, but on the day the contributions were to be received (which was the last day before the Christmas vacation), there was a terrible blizzard, and school was canceled. With snow and ice everywhere, no buses were running. But this thirteen-year-old boy was convinced there would be someone at the school to receive his money, so he walked through the blizzard and put his fifteen cents into the hands of the principal. As the boy turned to go back out into the blizzard to head back home, the principal had to swallow hard and blink back the tears, because the principal knew that this boy's name was on the list of underprivileged children who were to receive gifts from the Santa's Helpers Fund.

31

Isn't that beautiful? The power of sacrificial love, the power of loving others. What a great gift to bring to the Christmas stable at the inn.

As we come to the manger at Bethlehem today, we can do that too. We can bring the Christ Child three good gifts: our penitence, our gratitude, and our love for others. Or, in other words, *What can we give him? We can give him our hearts!*

## Questions for Reflection and Discussion

1. How do you select the perfect gift for someone? What are memorable gifts (these may include time, love, hope, and faith, for example) that others have given you?
2. Why were the three gifts from the wise men appropriate gifts for Jesus?
3. What does it mean to be penitent? In what ways can you show penitence to God in word and in deed?
4. If we are truly grateful to God, how should we respond through our actions?
5. Give reasons why love is the perfect gift.

## Prayer

Dear God, thank you for the many gifts you give to us each day. Thank you for food, clothing, shelter, family, friends, health, work, and so much more. You have blessed us with the gift of life. Help us truly appreciate it and make the most of it by giving of ourselves to you and to others. May we give love to the unloved and hope to the hopeless. Open our eyes to the needs of others, and help us respond in love. Amen.

## Focus for the Week

This week is about giving. Reflect on and pray about what God has given you, and what you can give back to God and others. Practice giving yourself away. Give of your time, your love, your patience, and your understanding. Be a good listener for someone who is feeling hurt or alone. Give a smile to someone who needs it. You are blessed by God; look for ways to share your blessings with others.

# The Miracle of Christmas

*Scripture: Read Matthew 1:18-25.*

Recently, I saw a Christmas card that fascinated me. At first glance, it looked very much like any other traditional Christmas card. On the front of the card was an exquisite print of a fifteenth-century painting by a noted Italian artist named Ghirlandaio. It depicted beautifully the manger scene on that silent and holy night so long ago. But a closer look revealed that this Christmas card was different from any other I had ever seen.

Mary and the baby Jesus are the most prominent figures in the painting. The Christ Child is lying on a bed of straw, with the radiant light of the Bethlehem star shining down on him. Mary is kneeling behind him. She is wearing a beautiful blue robe, her hands are clasped in a gesture of prayer, and her face is the picture of gratitude and serenity and adoration.

To the right are the shepherds. One of the shepherds is holding a lamb tenderly to his chest, anticipating, undoubtedly, Jesus' role as "the Lamb of God who takes away the sin of the world" (John 1:29). Over to the left, some townspeople are coming up a road from the nearby city, obviously coming to the manger to worship the newborn King.

In the background are the animals: an ox, a donkey, a goat, a lamb. But what caught my eye was Joseph. Now, get this—the shepherds are on one side, and Mary and the Christ Child are in the foreground. The townspeople are coming up from the left side. The animals are scattered all around, and everyone in the painting is looking at the baby Jesus. Everyone, that is, except Joseph.

Joseph is in the background. He is looking up into heaven with this quizzical look on his face, and he is scratching his head! I would imagine that scratching your head back then meant the same thing it does now. It means, "I don't get it!" "What in the world is going on here?" "What in the world is happening?" "What in the world does this mean?"

The great thing about Joseph is that even though he didn't understand all of what was going on at that first Christmas, nevertheless he accepted it and he celebrated it. Even though he was somewhat bewildered by it all, he trusted God and embraced Christmas. He welcomed the Christ Child into his life with open arms.

So can we. So should we. We are so like Joseph. We can't possibly comprehend the full meaning of Christmas. Christmas comes to us wrapped in divine mystery and wonder and awe. We can't master the fullness of Christmas in five simple steps or four easy lessons. But we don't have to. Like Joseph, all we need to do is to embrace Christmas, and celebrate Christmas, and welcome the Christ Child into our lives with open arms.

Recently a good friend gave me a fascinating article about the origin of the song "The Twelve Days of Christmas." According to the article, that popular song has a hidden meaning. It was written during a time of persecution to help children learn and remember the faith. The people were not permitted to practice their faith openly, so the song was designed to have two meanings—a surface meaning, and another, a hidden meaning known only to the people of faith. As you may remember, the song refers to gifts "my true love gave to me." They were taught the phrase "my true love gave to me" symbolized God and his love for us. See how well you can do in guessing the hidden meanings.

- The Partridge in the Pear Tree: Christ's death on the cross.
- Two Turtle Doves: The Old and New Testaments.
- Three French Hens: Faith, Hope, and Love.
- Four Calling Birds: Matthew, Mark, Luke, and John, the four Gospels.
- Five Golden Rings: The Torah, the first five books of the Bible.
- Six Geese a-laying: The six days of Creation.
- Seven Swans a-swimming: Seven gifts from the Holy Spirit.

- Eight Maids a-milking: The eight Beatitudes.
- Nine Ladies dancing: The nine Fruits of the Spirit.
- Ten Lords a-leaping: The Ten Commandments.
- Eleven Pipers piping: The eleven Faithful Disciples.
- Twelve Drummers drumming: The twelve Points of Belief in the Apostles' Creed.

I don't know how accurate this bit of trivia is, but it does make a point, namely this: there is usually a deeper meaning to most things! This is certainly true of Christmas. And even though we know up front that our human minds simply are not big enough to fully comprehend the fullness of what it means to say, "The Word became flesh and dwelt among us," still we need to stretch our minds and expand our souls and open our hearts to the deeper meanings of Christmas.

So, let's take a deep breath and take a shot at this: *What in the world is Christmas all about?* So many things! Christmas is about so many things that defy description, so many things too big for words. But for now, let me suggest three basic things that we can get our arms around, three things that Christmas is all about.

## First of All, Christmas Is the Reminder That God Is with Us Come What May

A few years ago, a woman wrote one of those Christmas letters, the kind that brings you up-to-date on what's happening in the family. It was the first Christmas since her husband had died, and she wrote about it. She knew that her friends would want to know how she was getting along. She was straightforward and honest about it all.

In her letter, she talked openly about the pain, the sorrow, the loneliness, and how tough it had been. Then she said this: "Now, I wonder about many things. I wonder, how can it be that he who is gone somehow continues to live and minister to me and to the children? I wonder, how is it that in the midst of heartache I have found God and the power to keep on going? I wonder, how is it that as a result of this tragedy, old friendships are deepened and new friendships are formed?"

The woman ended the letter by saying that it's the mystery of Christmas that holds the answer. "Christmas," she wrote, "is the promise that God can be trusted to meet all of our needs," and, as she had personally discovered in her own grief experience, "to meet our needs in ways we would never imagine." The last words of the letter are powerful. Listen closely: "Some say that this first Christmas without my husband will be very painful. Probably it will be. But I know this: Without Christmas, my life would be impossible."

That's the kind of faith Christmas is about. Christmas reconnects us to the Power Source. The message of Christmas is *Emmanuel,* which means "God is with us" in every circumstance of life, and even, indeed, beyond this life. God is with us, and God is for us. That is the Christmas "good news of great joy." That is our faith, and that's what Christmas is all about.

## *Second, Christmas Is the Reminder That God Will Never Desert Us*

In recent years, the poem "Footprints in the Sand" has become well known and much loved. Sometimes when I feel down, or a little blah, or just need some reassurance, I go back and read it again. It restores my strength and gives me confident hope. The poem tells of a person who has a dream one night about walking with God on the beach. The dreamer looks back and sees two sets of footprints in the sand, but then the dreamer notices that in the toughest, most difficult times of life, there is just a single set of footprints. The dreamer asked God, "How could You leave me in the worst times of my life?" And God answers, "O my precious child, I am always with you. I would never leave you. Those hard moments were the times I carried you!"

This is the message of Christmas, isn't it? And again the word is *Emmanuel.* God realizes that we need help, that we need someone to carry us, and he sends a Savior. And in so doing, God gives us the Christmas gift of hope, the Christmas gift of his presence, the Christmas promise that he will never desert us or forsake us.

Some years ago, a powerless submarine sank off the coast of New England. Rescue ships were rushed to the scene. Divers went down to see if they could rescue the submarine's crewmembers. The crewmembers clung to life as their oxygen supply was depleted.

The divers and the crewmembers inside the sub tapped out Morse code to communicate. The situation was more precarious the more time passed. After a pause, the crewmembers slowly tapped out: "Is there any hope?" The answer of Christmas to that question is a resounding yes, because God is with us, and he will not desert us.

## Third and Finally, Christmas Is the Reminder That God Is Love, and That God Wants Us to Be Loving

Some time ago, I was having lunch with some dear friends. One of them said, "Jim, have you heard the 'Orange Story'?" I hadn't, so, she told it to me, and I'm so glad she did. It's wonderful.

The story happened during the time of the Great Depression, in the 1930s. Eleven little boys were living in an orphanage. They were so poor. The highlight of their lives came each year on Christmas Eve. After their dinner in the orphanage cafeteria, they would have a Christmas party. They would sing some carols, and then each of the eleven boys would receive an orange. That's all they would get for Christmas—no toys, no clothes, no candy—just a single orange. But the little boys were so grateful. Each one would peel his orange carefully and eat one slice a day to make it last longer.

But one year on Christmas Eve, one little boy named Tommy broke one of the orphanage rules. The orphanage director said to him, "Tommy, you have broken one of our rules, and you must be disciplined. I hate to do it, but you have to learn, so your punishment is that you can't come to the Christmas party this year, and you won't get an orange. Go to your room immediately, and stay there until morning."

Tommy was crushed. He was so disappointed, but he obeyed. He went to his room alone. He could hear the sounds of the Christmas party. He could hear them singing; he could hear his friends cheer as the oranges were passed around. Tommy was absolutely heartsick. This was the lowest, darkest, worst moment of his life. He had trouble going to sleep at first, but finally sleep came.

When Tommy woke up the next morning, he sat on the edge of his bed rubbing his eyes and thinking, *This is going to be the most horrible Christmas ever.* But then he saw it. There it was, on the bedside table: a makeshift orange; an orange with no peel; ten individual slices of orange put together to make an orange for him. There was a note underneath it that read "Merry Christmas, Tommy," and it was signed by all ten of his friends. It took a moment for it all to sink in, but finally Tommy figured it out. Each one of his little buddies had donated one slice of their orange to make an orange for him, and what had started out to be Tommy's worst Christmas suddenly became his best Christmas ever! Sacrificial love turned it around for Tommy, and that's what Christmas is all about.

Now, let me ask you something. Where did those little boys learn to share like that? Where did they learn to give sacrificially like that? Where did they learn to redeem a situation creatively like that? Where did they learn to love like that? You know, don't you? They learned it from the Christmas Story. They learned it from those Christmas carols. But most of all, they learned it from the Christ Child, this One who came to visit and redeem; this One who came to save; this One who came to give his life sacrificially for you and me.

Let me ask you something else. Can you love like that? Can you love sacrificially like that? Can you? The poet put it like this: "For Christ is born and born again, / When his love lives in the hearts of men."

When we celebrate the good news that God is with us come what may, that God will never desert us, and that God is Love and wants us to be loving, then we have Christmas—a Christmas that will last all year long.

## Questions for Reflection and Discussion

1. How have your thoughts about the meaning of Christmas changed or remained the same over time?
2. In what ways does Christmas reconnect us with God?
3. The author points out that God is with us in every circumstance of life. When do you feel closest to God?
4. God will never desert us or forsake us; how should that fact change the way we live?
5. In your own words, describe the meaning of sacrificial love. How does Christmas remind us of this kind of love?

## Prayer

Dear God, thank you for leading us through Advent and preparing us for a more meaningful and joyous Christmas. May we celebrate the birth of Jesus in our hearts and remember why Christ came to earth. Thank you for loving us and for always being with us. May we

share your loving goodness with others, this Christmas and through-
out the year. Amen.

## Focus for the Week

The focus this week is on final preparations. Are you prepared for
the birth of Christ? Are you ready to share God's love and hospitality with others? How are you making the birth of the Christ Child the
central focus of your Christmas celebration? Take time to enjoy this
beautiful season of the year. This Christmas is another gift from God
to you.